AWAKENING
PERCEPTION

AWAKENING PERCEPTION

Poetry of a Toltec Warrior

To Rob + Marsha-

:) BE HAPPY!

Laura Barrette Shannon

Laura Barrette Shannon

To order additional copies of this book, contact:
Xlibris Corporation
1-888-795-4274
www.Xlibris.com
Orders@Xlibris.com
31678

Contents

I dedicate this book to my grandmother,
Gabrielle Riecke,
For teaching me to love words.

Introduction

My poetry is a reflection of my philosophical thoughts and continuing journey of awakening. I follow the path with a heart, that of a Toltec warrior. This is a life long process of exploring awareness and expanding perception. I have been most influenced by the great works of don Miguel Ruiz and Carlos Castaneda. Their words are ripples flowing through space and time, gently washing upon my mind, helping to clear my filters of perception. I extend my eternal gratitude to these great warriors.

Of course, I have also been influenced by my personal life experiences. I battled my own mortality through a disabling health condition for many years, before a life saving brain surgery helped ease my physical pain and brought back my mental ability to think clearly. This coincided with the accidental death of my only daughter at age eleven, in the fall of 2000.

These traumatic experiences provided a climate of deep philosophic introspection of life, spirituality, and myself. In the process, I befriended my past, found purpose and began to see life as perfectly beautiful for the first time. Now, I have peace of mind and happiness. I truly enjoy each moment of my being.

I think you will find my poetry to be thought provoking and possibly a tool for your own personal transformation.

BE GREAT!

Laura Barrette Shannon
November 07, 2005

Acknowledgments

I would like to extend my eternal gratitude to the many teachers who have touched my life. This list includes all of the people who I have ever known and all whose words have brushed upon my mind, adding to the artistic tapestry of my thoughts. I would like to extend special thanks to the following people who helped make this book possible:

To my brother, Jerry Smith, my mentor and friend, for being a great inspiration and a model of a well balanced life.

To my friend, John Jendzejec, for demonstrating the power of intent and creation through his life.

To my son, Rick Barrette, for teaching me the virtues of patience, and introducing me to Allpoetry.com.

To my sister, Christine Charbonneau, for always being there for me when I need her. Our Sunday Scrabble games were a lifeline when I was drowning in grief.

To my friends, Liz Anderson, Pam Ajitomi, and Dawn Brew, for their continuing encouragement and friendship.

To my friends at Allpoetry.com, especially Presence, and Doug Crandall, for their constant support and encouragement of my work.

And to my best friend, companion, and husband, Ray Shannon, for literally saving my life.

I love and honor each of you for the blessings you have brought me-

Laura

The Space Between
Nov 1, 2005

The wise man knows how little he understands;
the fool understands little of what he knows.
To know the unknowable,
to understand the incomprehensible,
this is the quest of many a life.
Who has the power to see through the illusions
to the space between the lines
of those limited questions of the mind?
This is the one who knows
how little he understands,
because he can truly see.

Abundance
Apr 24, 2003

You can not own
a shimmering sunset,
or crystal stars of night.
You can not own
a brilliant blowing breeze,
or the spark of sweet sunlight.

You can not keep
a fragrant floral scent,
or an infant's sleepy sigh.
You can not keep
love's first embrace,
or life's ecstatic highs.

You can not possess
that time which went by
before you were even born.
You can not possess
those memories made
long after you are gone.

So experience enjoyment
in each moment,
immerse in sight, sense, and sound.
Appreciate this world
for all that it is,
that's where abundance is found.

Rippling Waves
Jul 21, 2003

Like a pebble dropped into a pond
our lives affect many, today and beyond,
causing ripples with what we say
in those we touch throughout the day.
One kind word or action well done
can change the world for someone.
Our thoughts, opinions, and attitudes
are absorbed by all, influencing moods.
Never underestimate the power of words,
'cause what is said is always heard,
rippling waves through space and time,
so keep speech positive and actions kind.

Spring Rain
Jun 06, 2003

The spring rain falls gently down,
like a warm sprinkling shower,
seeping Earth with soothing sound,
erasing time until this hour.

Fearlessly, flowers face this day,
while I'm wallowing wet with doubts.
Drenched and dripping I drop to pray
among the fresh emerging sprouts.

Ah . . . Pure power pours into me!
Washing away my private pain.
Restoring peace and serenity,
quenching my thirst for life again.

Silence
Aug 20, 2003

Silence . . .

quietly sings
breathes peace
frees thought
brings release

Silence . . .

connects one
to the source
allows unity
guides course

Silence . . .

relaxes mind
clears chatter
relieves worry
so fears shatter

Silence . . .

charges soul
renews self
taps knowledge
of innate wealth

I Am
Oct 10, 2003

I am a spark of light from the sun
leaving the source
separating
forgetting
the ONE.

I am the seasons flowing through time
living the illusion
playing
laughing
crying

I am the shaper of all that be
experiencing life
creating
dreaming
reality

I am the rain falling into the sea
joining the source
merging
remembering
me

My Brother
Nov 1, 2003

When life beat me down, you taught me to stand,
leading the way, but not holding my hand.
When I sought advice you shared your insight,
but then you would add, "Go do as you might."

You stood by me through life's good and bad,
Inspiring hope when I was so sad.
You encouraged depth, to learn how to see
the innate potential deep inside of me.

I discovered myself, and befriended my past
finding life's lessons from birth until last.
I strived to be strong in body and mind
I learned most of all to always be kind.

Now that I'm wiser, I clearly see
this life is my own; I can set myself free!
Creating health, wealth, happiness and peace
by power within which you helped release.

New Beginnings
Dec 20, 2003

There is no death
only new beginnings
transmuting energy
forever flowing through time
dynamically evolving spirits
eternally incarnating
an infinitely transforming force
of universal creation.

Truth in Paradox
Mar 20, 2004

We are all *One*,
yet also unique individuals,
separate yet united;
ever perfect,
yet constantly changing,
in dynamic evolution,
eternally here,
now, before, and tomorrow,
all at the same time,
which does not exist . . .

Choose To Be
Dec 31, 2003

I am now whom I choose to be,
consciously guiding my destiny.
I once blamed fate for loosing my way,
but my past actions formed today.
I was asleep; slumbering through life;
dreaming daily; seeding strife.
Now, I pick, plan and persist,
intending to be whom I insist.
I duel demons; I fight my fear,
with actions as my weapons;
thoughts as my seer,
I will endure until the end,
minding each moment that I spend,
knowing that I'm forever free,
to be whom I choose to be.

The Parasite
Jul 21, 2003

You have no power over me!
Thought you'd beat me down
with your wounding words,
trying to drain my energy.

You have no power over me!
Thought you'd cast doubts,
cloud my mind with worry,
never let me be.

You have no power over me!
Though your persistent chatter
can be challenging to ignore,
I will continue to be free!

Remember
Aug 26, 2004

Remember . . .
There is no one path to take,
experience the journey-
stay awake.

Remember . . .
When life is full of pain
look for the lesson
or repeat again.

Remember . . .
Time changes all things,
but by changing yourself
the unchangeable sings.

Remember . . .
What you ponder, say, and do,
are living prayers
answered on cue.

Remember . . .
Happiness is a state of mind,
trained by thoughts-
the loving kind.

Remember . . .
When dark emotions emerge,
by reacting with patience
control will surge.

Remember . . .
Before you even ask "Why?"
Answer the question:
Who am I?

My Captain
Jan 27, 2003

Waves of thought, crashing,
crashing through my mind,
breaking on the rocks
at the edge of clarity.

Where is my Captain?

Winds of confusion, blowing,
blowing uncontrollably.
Dark storms of twisted thoughts
slowly sinking serenity.

Where is my Captain?

Through wind and salt, searching,
searching to break free,
'tis then I find who feeds my fate,
guiding me through life's sea.

I'm my own Captain!

I will ride with the tide,
set sail with the wind,
steer towards the brightest star,
forging the flow of destiny!

Voices in My Head
Mar 06, 2004

I hear these voices in my head,
"Don't open your eyes." "Stay in bed."
Sleep on my mind, the darkness sets,
now caught deep in depression's nets.

How can I go on? Win this fight?
What weapon yields this demon's might?
Can I ride this storm in my soul,
slay this demon, once and for all?

Heeding his words, gives him power,
busying my mind for an hour,
will save my precious energy,
give me the weapon to break free.

I'll face this demon without fear.
I'll draw my sword; the end will near.
Ignore those voices in my head,
I'll slay this demon! Now he's dead!

What Dreams May Come
May 17, 2005

My list changes with the seasons,
And grows with the passing years,
I reflect upon it often,
Penning plans, I'm my own seer.

From time to time I'll battle demons,
Fight my social phobias and such,
I'll try not to make assumptions,
And not take things personally as much.

Someday I'll buy a little camper,
And follow both wind and whim,
Connect with wonderful people and places,
In the sea of life I'll swim.

I'll meditate under the magnificent Redwoods,
Hike up a majestic mountain or two,
Wallow in healing hot springs,
And bask in the glorious Grand Canyon view.

I'll dwell in a multitude of places,
But, wherever I am will be home,
I'll enjoy a long happy marriage,
But someday I'll walk alone.

I'll expose my soul to the world,
And oust the ego from my mind,
I'll learn to love myself as I Am,
Finding opportunities to be kind.

I'll be blissful and content just being,
True to my own self and heart,
Never hide behind false masks,
And finish whatever I start.

I'll arise many morns to the lull of the sea,
Tasting the salt of serenity's song,
Practice yoga on the beach with sand in my toes,
To keep my body stretched and strong.

I'll help heal many bodies and souls,
By sharing divine energy;
I'll listen, teach, and console,
Ever inspiring seekers to see.

I'll experience my inner greatness,
Because I'll always do my best,
I'll stand by my soul's convictions,
And not worry about the rest.

I'll know awe at the Arora Borealis,
And merge with the mind of ONE,
Ponder life in reflective lunar light,
And read numerous books in the sun.

I'll experience enjoyment in each moment,
Indulge in sight, sense, and sound,
Explore marvelous magical places,
And visit mystical realms yet found.

I'll poetically express my philosophy
And thoughts, into eloquent poems and prose,
Weaving words with love and integrity,
In all of the work I compose.

As I traverse the path with a heart,
I'll know my personal freedom,
By expanding awareness and perception,
I'll welcome what dreams may come.

I intend to experience so much more,
More than I can imagine this day,
So, I'll be back to add to this list,
But for now, it's for these things I pray . . .

For This I Pray
Dec 16, 2004

For this I pray,

Let my life
reflect your love,
like the light of the sun,
shining on those
still in darkness.

Let my life
grow in your compassion,
like the mighty oak,
shading those who
need understanding.

Let my life
experience your peace,
like a dove flying free,
comforting those who
are heavy with grief.

Let my life
be one with your will,
like an extended hand,
helping those who
pray for your guidance.

Amen

The Awakening
Aug 19, 2004

PART I

Once, when my life seemed so sad and so dark,
I had lost life's purpose and spirit's spark.
Confidence of youth, once had, was now gone,
I felt so empty inside, so alone.
Why did I allow life to beat me down?
How can lost faith ever be found?
Silently, I thought, life was never fair,
If this were the end, I just wouldn't care.
My life was but a movie replaying
Over again. Still hearing her saying,
"I love you, Mom. I'll be home next week."
Her sweet words repeated as I fell to sleep.
Little did I know those prophetic words;
I never expected what next I heard.

RING . . . RING . . . .

Springing awake, ring breaking silent night,
Bringing my worst unimaginable fright,
Ringing my heart with unspeakable fear,
Unable to speak . . . or hide anywhere . . .

This must be a dream!! It simply can't be!!
I didn't create this reality!
I can't even breathe!! I can't even think!
My whole life destroyed in one of God's winks!

Silent screams echo his words in my head,
Unable to process those words he said.
Why would this happen to one still so young?
Life's potential song left sadly unsung.

Her body was shipped home, cold, but on time,
Irony fulfilled, with her destined last line.

The Awakening
Aug 19, 2005

·PART II

Days turned to weeks, as the seasons flew by,
Shadowy dark storms hid light from my eyes.
I pondered my life; Its meaning unclear:

Could I ever awake? Leave this nightmare?
Why did this happen? It didn't seem right.
I don't have the strength to battle this fight.
There must be some reason; lesson to find.
Was life pre-ordained? Destiny designed?
Could my soul evolve by suffering pain?
Would it be better, to just go insane?

I wanted to give up, to lay down and die.
I drank every night, most days I'd just cry.
I had plenty of time to think and to read.
I started to see *intent* was a seed!

Forming my intent, I planted peace of mind,
Purpose would soon follow, not far behind.
I chose patience, as a good place to start
To regain some power, warm up my heart.

After some time, on one special day,
Peace of mind came, so life wasn't so gray.
The purpose of life, for me, was to grow.
I then understood how to love and let go.

My time in hell was just a catalyst,
Pressuring me 'til I couldn't resist,
Fates loud, pounding bell, ringing in my soul,
Jarring me awake with destiny's call.

In Memory of Nicole Barrette 1988-2000

I Am Many Things
Mar 18, 2005

My essence is love, but I have many roles:

I am . . .
a parent with a very patient hand,
the friend who's always there to understand,
a sibling to all of mankind,
the lover of life, all hearts wish to find,
a teacher when the ready student appears,
the student who's ever ready to hear,
a warrior of the Toltec way,
the light beyond on a cloudy day,
an example of how one can grow,
the hope in a bright rainbow,
a slave to the opinions of none,
the joy in a job well done,
an embodied spark of light,
the peace, not just the might.

I play these parts and many more too;
I'll fill many roles before I am through.

The Chair
Mar 23, 2005

I slowly recline in the chair,
Which warmly awaits me each time I visit,
Soft music and stillness engulf the room.
I try to relax, lose myself in the melodies
and just stare at the faint watermark above me.

But . . . my thoughts of peace are interrupted by
The sweet metallic taste of blood,
And the harsh grating sounds, scraping,
Scraping, clearing away indulgent sins
Right down to the bone.

Then, just when the discomfort is overwhelming,
I remember why I come to this chair,
For I am a willing participant in this bi-annual
Cleansing ritual, restoring and refreshing
My beautiful white smile.

Oh, Little Child
Nov 20, 2005

Oh, little child of mine,
searching for wisdom,
seeking to find,
asking me questions,
about life and death,
sharing your *love*
with every breath . . .
How can I tell you,
what words can be said,
the answers you seek
are inside your head,
for *love* is the answer
to all questions posed.
Remember your essence,
be open not closed.
Reach for the stars,
dance and be free,
be the *love* that you are
for the whole world to see.

Transmutation
Apr 24, 2005

May my pride
turn outward,
in awe of God,
in love with life itself.

May my envy
transmute into inspiration
pushing me toward that
which I yearn to be.

May my gluttonous nature
drive me to
consume each moment
with intense awareness.

May my lust
for passion
power my quest
for divine wisdom.

May my anger
quickly prompt me
to be patient with others,
my life and myself.

May my greediness
be met with a desire
to share all that
I have been given.

May my slothfulness
remind me to
appreciate the silence
in just . . . being.

The Calling
Nov 2, 2004

Shh . . .

*Words of whispered love
ring within my soul!*

*Calling me to
awaken!*

*Arousing
my spirit!*

*Reminding me to
embrace
my holiness
and remember
my
wholeness!*

What Is Real
Aug 20, 2004

In this world of chaotic change,
I am at peace.
Breath
of tranquility
calms my restless
mind.
Just *being*
present
blocks emotional
turmoil,
reminding me
what is
real.

The Miracle
Nov 2, 2004

As I look around,
I see myself,
disguised as many,
reflected in all.

I see my imagined
faults and weaknesses,
embodied in my deception,
woven into my perception,
constantly mirroring
my beliefs about myself.

The Miracle is this:

Forgiveness!

Offering me opportunities
to express my loving essence
and be One with the will
of Love.

For by forgiving all,
I forgive myself,
releasing my own guilt.
With my guilt gone,
atonement is complete,
allowing me to awaken
to my Wholeness.

The Last Day
Aug 25, 2004

When upon my heart's last beat
I know I will leave willingly,
Embracing death, as I have life,
With honor and integrity.

Knowing well how I lived my days,
With intended purpose and principle,
Aspiring toward the common good
While smiling on all people.

I do not know if that day is soon,
So I'll waste no time to be!
Loving life and enjoying all
'till I set my spirit free.

White Rabbit
Sept 08, 2004

Would you dare to follow the white rabbit, glance through the looking glass, knowing your world would become a magical realm, a surreal wonderland, where nothing is as it seems, and everything is nothing?

Would you let go of nothing to gain everything? Did you ever think you'd have to lose your mind to find your soul? Forget your identity to remember who you are?

Do you know how to embrace the darkness to restore the light? Accept hell to reclaim heaven?

Do you have ears to hear the deafening truth in the resounding silence? Or the vision to see through your disabling self serving blindness?

Will you ever shut the book of knowledge, with its symbolic worldly words and learn the ways of wisdom?

Could you forgive everything for not appearing perfect, even though it is?

I am just wondering . . .

What if Love does not make the world go round, but could actually be the source of awakening from this cosmic circle of life? Love being outside the eternal loop of time, before the beginning, without end. Love unconditionally unifying all, until ultimately the disillusioned universe disappears, like a distant dream . . .

Reality
May 07, 2005

Right here, right now,
Each in our own perceptual dream,
A holographic virtual universe,
Life manifesting into existence,
Influenced by our intentions,
Twinkling in and out of time,
Yesterday as unreal as tomorrow.

Worry
May 08, 2005

Wracking thoughts and wasted energy,
On negative outcomes of future events,
Replaying fearful scenarios over and over,
Ruining peaceful serenity and even
Yielding possible self fulfilling tragedy.

Happiness
May 09, 2005

Having perpetual peace of mind by
Allowing life to naturally flow,
Putting worries out of your thoughts,
Practicing emotional self control
In all stressful situations,
Never judging or assuming anything,
Ever diligently forgiving everything,
Silencing the ego's cacophonous chatter,
Seeing life as perfectly beautiful.

Integrity
Nov 13, 2005

Inner moral character, developed from honor and respect
Not being self centered, focused on unity and wholeness
Trusting in the divine Tao, knowing life has purpose
Ethical in all endeavors, in all spheres of being
Going with the flow, not against the grain
Raising the bar of probity toward the highest apex
Integrating truth and honesty into scrupulous mastery
Training the mind, body, and soul, building self esteem
Yearning to always act for the greater good

Flowers
Jun 06, 2005

As the morning sun rises out of the east,
I hear light beams shout out of the darkness,
I see the flowers begin to forget the cool night
as they blossom forth to greet dawn's daily illumination.

Without fear, they face each moment of their being,
filled with beautiful acceptance of life,
they humbly bow their heads in respect to the rain
and they do not fight the winds of change.

Each night, they passively sleep with serenity,
unscathed by the shadows of life's worries,
unlike men, who so often choose to suffocate themselves,
drowning nightly in the waters of their dark speculations.

Is it the bliss of ignorance or their natural innocence,
which soothes their slumber each night?
Or is it their faith in God and the seasonal circle of life,
which allows them such courage to face each day?

Sands of Time
Jun 24, 2005

The sands of time are speaking,
whispering their ancient wonders.
Can we hear the voice of the Sphinx,
In the resounding cries of thunder?

In the repetitive errs of the past
can we see humanity's fate?
In the burning cries of the forests,
will we listen before it's too late?

In the gasp of poisoned waters,
which are too dark to even swim,
will we justify our own pollution
thinking "It's not us. It's them."?

Choking through the asthmatic smog
Can we see where responsibility begins?
Will we ever understand the signs,
and stop our self-destructive sins?

An Owl' s Presence
Nov 02, 2005

As the grand luminous ball of light
commences its ritualistic rise,
a fledgling owl flutters silently . . .
gliding into my hypnotic gaze,
landing on the fence. He can see me,
yet he is still . . .
recognizing a friend,
he proudly sits, steadily staring,
twisting his inquisitive head, from side to side
intently watching for a scampering mouse,
or stealthy feline predator.

Oh, wise bird!
You grace me with your presence,
allowing me the pleasure
of perceiving your beauty,
while I breathe with gentle exhilaration,
seeing . . .
experiencing . . .
the sunrise
for the first time.

Flying with the Gods
Jul 08, 2005

Through the eyes of this steel eagle,
I am blessed with divine vision!

Behold!
The vast snowy sea of foam
swirling beneath my soaring spirit,
waves of gray shadowed valleys
mingled with white shimmering peaks,
bubbling, glistening,
gently metamorphosing
into a myriad of imaginary images . . .

High above this heavenly phenomenon,
I hover in wondrous splendor,
removed; I start to remember . . .
Is this not what the ancient Gods observed
from their world beyond our perception?
Was Mount Olympus made of such beautiful
translucent vapors, boundlessly
interconnected, eternally materializing
into resplendent shapes and forms?

But wait! Look!
Beyond my upper threshold of sight,
I ascend yet higher,
higher;
I break through toward the light!
What shimmering brilliance,
illumination,
emanating an iridescent glow,
in a plethora of pastel shades,
heightening my senses,
enlightening
my conscious contemplation . . .

Within this surreal landscape,
there is an occasional window,
a transparent gateway.
Like Jupiter and Juno
I intently scry through the porthole,
a looking glass perspective
into the realm of mere mortal existence,
a glimpse into the lives of those whom
are still grounded and have yet to fly.

In a glorious gaze,
I glance at the Earth,
its veins of rivers and roads
appearing so distant . . .
a forgotten scene in a childhood dream.
People mindlessly moving,
working, sleep walking through life,
never giving thought to the awesome
workings of the heavens above . . .

Through this unobstructed vista,
I continue my ascension,
propelling higher,
higher,
until I finally transcend the feint fog
of misty memories
and for one magical moment . . .
My perception is perfectly clear!
Life below this point
is so minuscule . . . irrelevant . . .

ALL that is, is NOW!
ONE lofty moment in time
where I am flying free!
Free of Earthly gravitation,
Free of the daily grinding burdens of life,
Free to let my consciousness soar,
Free to feel heavenly exaltation,
with the divine vision of the Gods.

I Believe
Nov 13, 2004

I believe in Love,
the infinite power that binds
the Universal force
that seekers hope to find.

I believe in Life,
the experience to be
our free will to choose
is the only hidden key.

I believe in Light,
the eternal force of One,
energetic transformations
forming Father into Son.

I believe in Heaven,
the salvation of the soul
attained by self-forgiveness-
resurrection of the Whole.

I believe in Hell,
imagined torments of the mind,
believing lies are real,
alone, fearful, and blind.

I believe in Peace,
the compassion in all things,
that wisdom to recognize
what the common good could bring.

Diamond in the Rough
Sept 20, 2005

Do not judge me by my foolish
actions of youth and yesterday,
rather, see me now,
as the woman I have become.
Realize that each wrong turn taken
has gently cut its mark,
chipping away at ignorance.
Every phase and facet of my life
has honed my perception,
refining my wisdom,
revealing my genuine spirit,
allowing it to sparkle forth
as radiant light upon the world
like a dazzling diamond!

Moonlit Shadows
Sept 08, 2005

Under the moonlit shadows,
Beneath the sycamore tree,
Wind through the weeping willows
Whisks up old memories.

I know I could not stay behind,
That would have meant my demise.
I needed to follow my heart and mind,
follow my truth, face the good-byes.

My destiny lied upon a different shore,
My future forged by my own hands,
I desired to open distant doors,
To begin exploring bigger plans.

Under the moonlit shadows,
My memories dance into the breeze,
I feel the invigorating breath of life
I live here, now, content, and pleased.

Where the Road Turns
Jul 07, 2005

Come! Follow me,
Where the road turns,
'Cause I'll be moving on
To where my heart yearns.

Come! Be with me,
Where the road shifts,
Find the path to peace
By accepting life's gifts.

Come! Follow me,
Where the road turns,
The healing hands of time
Will ease those past burns.

Come! Be with me
Where the road bends
Try a different path
Find out where it ends.

Come! Follow me
Where the road turns,
Don't get left behind
In your past concerns.

Come! Be with me
Where the road twists
We'll have so much fun,
We'll learn to live in bliss!

The Sitting Stone
Sept 20, 2005

Beside the rolling waves,
down near the depth of the sea,
when you feel the need to relax,
to recharge your energy,

Come,
bring only yourself,
sit,
discover your place,
feel
the refreshing wind
through your hair,
upon your face.

I'll never drain you,
or judge you at all.

I'll listen
to your heart sing,
and hear
your soul's call.

Stop,
watch the gulls soar,
as they fly
to and fro,
for they hold a great secret,
Search,
and you will know.

Breathe . . .
taste the seasoning of life
in the salty ocean air,
preserving precious time,
in this moment,
we share.

Breathe . . .
smell the fresh aroma-
nature's permeating scent,
surrounding us,
wholly,
NOW,
and each moment.

Breathe . . .
Shh . . . listen close,
if you're quiet
you'll hear
the sounds of eternity,
in constant flux,
everywhere.

Breathe . . .
let go and feel
the invigorating light of the sun,
sense the power
within;
then you'll connect
with the
ONE.

I'll be waiting for you,
Anytime, any day,
Whenever you need to recharge,
just come here,
sit and stay.

Seeds of Destiny
Sept 10, 2005

Perhaps destiny is an unchangeable seed,
as an acorn can be naught but an oak tree.
Yet, maybe fate is only a default design,
the shape of its growth in our own mind.

Perhaps destiny is woven in such a way
which allows our inner intentions to sway
the ultimate path which the branches will take,
each branch a choice that free will makes.

And, if we can prune away our faults,
eliminate that which slows the waltz,
our limbs will gladly dance towards the light,
awaking love by day, dreaming life by night.

If this proposition of fate holds true,
then we should act impeccably in all we do.
We need to be wise, nurture our fate,
by acting with integrity in all we create.

The Wheel of Chance
Nov 01, 2004

Be it fortune or fate,
The wheel of chance will turn,
Opening a new gate,
For what intention yearns.

What moves this wheel of chance?
Sometimes a friend or foe,
Swings life's familiar dance
Changing the world we know.

Life changes offer new schemes,
When Lady luck appears,
To aptly answer your dreams,
Just be your own seer.

The wheel of chance will spin
In each and every life.
Watch that wheel, then begin
Wielding destiny's knife.

Carve your fate, turn the wheel,
Take opportunities;
See the chance life reveals
Shift your reality!

Universal Mirror
Mar 24, 2004

I
~
ONE
Light
reflects . . .
my perception
is formed by belief
born in me, unfolding my
inner self into my reality, wonder,
awe, amazement, is what I really AM, a
mystical, magical being in multidimensional lands.
I can not truly explain this outer world I see until I truly
understand the Universe in me, each atom a reflection,
of the world's perfection, electrons orbiting,
molecular Love bonding eternal energy,
forming my corporal body,
a Universal mirror,
reflecting the
Light of
ONE
~
I

My Ocean
July 21, 2005

Origin of life from which
Ancient creatures emerged,
Warm womb of Mother Earth,
Where swirling saline currents surge.

Enormous azure blue expanse
Surrounding continental lands,
Engulfing all aquatic life,
Home to seaweed, shells, and sand.

Mysterious depths within dark abyss,
Underwater mountain ranges,
Momentous waves move and crash,
Effected by lunar tidal changes.

The ocean is my sanctuary,
Where I return like rivers and rain,
Reminding me of the greater whole
From whence my soul once came.

ONE Perfection
Mar 29, 2005

Once . . .

ONE
Perfection

then . . .

the first speculation,
which started separation,
to experience exploration,
through dynamic evolution,
via infinite perceptions,
suffering self deception . . .

until . . .

an eventual reflection,
formed a vague recollection,
of remembered perfection,
a revealing revelation,
encouraging transformation,
allowing transfiguration,
into self unification,

and
ultimately . . .

ONE
Perfection

Phoenix Bird
May 07, 2005

There once was an unconventional philosopher
of highly controversial and disputed descent.
Some found his words repugnant and heretical,
while others listened to his parables with a delightful ear,
hearing more than mere tales, they understood
his cryptic yet precise message of love and peace.

Then, as one man hung from his tree of redemption,
the great philosopher of love was nailed to a cross,
starting thousands of thoughtful interpretations
of his life and words. Astounding ancient and modern
students with gnostic truth, encouraging them to love their
brothers, to dream of peace, and to follow the river of life
with an eternal smile, embracing each sunrise, as an awesome
symbol of renewal, Love resurrecting spirits
like the Phoenix bird rising!

Balance
Sept 03, 2005

balance
is key
to:

clarity
of
mind

vitality
of
body

tranquility
of
soul

each one
interconnected
and affected
by:

thoughts
of the
mind

actions
of the
body

and

feelings
of the
soul

Wood Burning
Aug 26, 2005

Is it the fragrance
of the freshly stoked fire,
the smooth smoky aroma
of pine and oak . . .

I can still smell your musky scent

Or is it the crackling,
snaps,
and pops,
bestowing animated voice
to the steady rumbling roar . . .

I can still hear our late night fireside chats

Or maybe it's the hypnotic dance
of the flames,
jumping,
crawling,
climbing,
from log to log . . .

I can still see the fire dancing in your eyes

Or perhaps,
it's the welcoming warmth
of the familiar heat,
stifling the bitterness
of cold,
leaving only the taste
of fond sweetness
burning,
in my memories
of you.

October
Oct 30, 2005

October begins the change,
each earthly hue emerges
brightly,
briefly,
before winter's cool twilight
brings only memories
of the colorful past.

Why can't the vibrancy
last a little longer?

Instead, some will float along
riding the high winds of hope
as far and as long as possible.

Some will depart in their own time,
fashionably falling,
happily landing close to their family.

While others will wither
while still on the tree of life,
frozen by the fear of fleeting
towards their death,
without ever knowing
the wonders of flight.

Author Notes

You may view and comment on my work at:

www.allpoetry.com/ToltecWarrior